The Gift of Life

Children's Book for the Eucharist

Anglican Church of Canada

This book belongs to

_____

given by

_____

It is the Lord's day!
Jesus invites us to his special meal. He says,

"Do this in memory of me"

We gather together

When we were baptized, we became members of God's Church. Now, here we are, gathered as a large family, united by our faith in Jesus.

In the name of the Lord who is present in our midst, the priest welcomes us:

The grace of our Lord Jesus Christ...

We reply: **And also with you.**

Sometimes we say together a prayer:

Almighty God,
to you all hearts are open...

Glory to God...

United in joy, we praise God with one heart by singing

> *Glory to God in the highest,*
> **and peace to his people on earth...**

or another song of praise.

We pray in silence, and then the priest says a short prayer called the collect to which we reply,

Amen.

We listen to God's Word

The Book of God's Word tells us the most beautiful story in the world, the Great Story of God's love for all the people of the earth.

In the beginning
there was God:
the Father, the Son,
and the Holy Spirit,
united in love
and happiness.
God wanted to share
that love and happiness...

So God created the Universe and all beings in it.

*God wanted the people of the world
to live as one happy family,
caring for the earth
and sharing its riches.
It was a beautiful dream!
It was a great hope for the world!*

But the people of the earth did not understand God's dream. They didn't want to share. They forgot about God and lost the way to happiness and friendship.

Over and over again the prophets warned people to return to the ways of God, and through them God renewed the promises of blessing and freedom.

In the first readings, God's friends tell us again about this Great Story. They also tell us what we have to do to find the way to happiness and friendship once more.

After these readings, we answer:
Thanks be to God.

Sometimes we sing or say a psalm.

Then we listen to the Gospel, the Good News about Jesus. To show our love and respect for the Lord, we stand and sing out our joy with a hymn.

The Lord be with you.
And also with you.
The Holy Gospel of our Lord Jesus Christ according to...
Glory to you, Lord Jesus Christ.

"A Saviour is born to you, it is Jesus, the Lord."

"Have trust, God loves you."

"Get up and walk."

"Go in peace, your sins are forgiven."

"Father, forgive them..."

"Father, I place my life in your hands."

"We have seen the Lord, he is risen!"
"We too, we recognized him when he broke the bread!"

At the end of the Gospel, we acclaim God's Word:
Praise to you, Lord Jesus Christ.

The priest helps us to understand God's Word for us today.

Here are some of Jesus' words to think about:

"When you are gathered in my name, I am with you."

"Happy are those who listen to God's Word and keep it in their heart!"

"All will know you are my friends if you love one another."

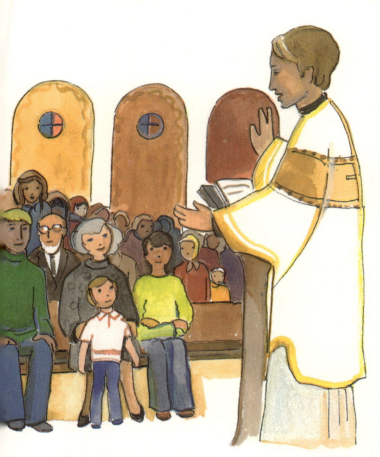

After the sermon, we stand to profess our faith:

**We believe in one God,
 the Father, the Almighty...
We believe in one Lord, Jesus Christ...
We believe in the Holy Spirit,
 the Lord, the giver of life...**

Let us pray to the Lord

There are people in our world
who are poor and hungry,
who have no work and no friends,
who are sad and lonely,
who are sick or wounded.

There are children who have
no home or no family.

At the eucharist we pray for all these people.

We pray also for the whole Church,
for the leaders of our countries
and all of us gathered here.
We ask for the courage to work
for justice and peace in the world:

Lord, hear our prayer.

We confess our sins...

In listening to Jesus, Zacchaeus becomes aware that he is a sinner and he wants to improve:
"Lord, I'm going to give back what I took and share the rest with the poor."

Jesus tells Zacchaeus:
"Today God's forgiveness has changed your heart."

and receive forgiveness

We too, like Zacchaeus,
are sinners. But we trust in God who
always forgives us. Together we say:

**Have mercy on us and forgive us,
that we may delight in your will,
and walk in your ways...**

Happy are those who make peace! They are truly God's children.

It is often hard to make peace.
Each day we have to start over.

But Jesus is there in other people
to help us, as the priest reminds us
by saying:

The peace of the Lord be always with you.

We answer:

And also with you.

Jesus asks us to be reconciled
before sharing the Bread of Life.

If you don't feel right with someone,
ask Jesus for the courage to make peace
and be reconciled in the next few days.

We prepare the bread and wine

God gives us the earth,
God gives us the sun and the rain,
God gives us the wheat and the grapes.

With the wheat and the grapes we make bread to nourish us and wine to give us joy.

We collect money for the work of the church and the needs of the world.

The priest prays over the gifts.

We reply: **Amen.**

O Lord, you do marvellous things for us,
you create us to be happy!
We praise and thank you:

The Lord be with you.
And also with you.
Lift up your hearts.
We lift them to the Lord.
Let us give thanks to the Lord our God.
It is right to give our thanks and praise.

Think of the joys
of this past week

and join your community
in giving thanks to God.

The most wonderful gift of God
is Jesus the Lord!

Through Jesus we know God our Father.
Through Jesus we receive the Spirit
and are guided on the way
of eternal life.

Because of God's great love for us
we give thanks, united with all of
God's friends on earth and in heaven:

**Holy, holy, holy Lord,
God of power and might,
heaven and earth are full of your glory.
Hosanna in the highest.**

**Blessed is he who comes
in the name of the Lord.
Hosanna in the highest.**

Continuing our prayer of thanksgiving, we remember what Jesus said and did during his last supper with his friends.

The priest says the words of Jesus:

*Take, and eat: this is my body
which is broken for you.*

*This is my blood which is shed
for you and for many. When you
do this, you do it in memory of me.*

Filled with hope because of Jesus who saves us,
we proclaim his presence among us.
We say an acclamation:

Glory to you for ever and ever.

The priest asks God our Father to make our gifts of bread and wine holy through the power of the Spirit.

We ask that the Spirit may fill our hearts with joy and help us grow together in love.

We pray for the renewal of the whole world, and that all the people of the earth may be gathered one day into God's house for the great feast of eternal life.

Along with the priest, offer to God with Jesus your everyday life:

your work and your play, your joys and your pains,

your efforts to grow and to love as he did.

*We sing your praise, almighty Father,
through Jesus, our Lord,
in the power of the Holy Spirit,
now and for ever.*

Glory to you for ever and ever. Amen.

We are all different, but all of us are God's children. We have received the same Spirit, the Spirit of Jesus, who teaches us to pray to God our Father:

**Our Father in heaven,
hallowed be your name,
your kingdom come,
your will be done,
on earth as in heaven.**

**Give us today our daily bread.
Forgive us our sins
as we forgive those who sin against us.
Save us from the time of trial,
and deliver us from evil.
For the kingdom, the power,
and the glory are yours,
now and for ever. Amen**

We break bread together

The priest breaks the bread
to remind us that we all share
the new life of Jesus.

We are invited to share in communion

The gifts of God for the People of God.

We reply: **Thanks be to God.**

Jesus comes to you
to help you live as a child of God,
to lead you on the way of eternal life.

Lord Jesus, my friend, I am coming to you.

The body of Christ, the bread of heaven.
Amen.

The blood of Christ, the cup of salvation.
Amen.

Jesus said:

"I am the bread of life. Whoever comes to me will never be hungry; whoever believes in me will never thirst."

Jesus is with you. Speak to him in your heart, as to your best friend.

Write here one or two prayers that you would like to say to Jesus after communion.

At the end of the eucharist
there is a short prayer and
sometimes a blessing.

Then we are dismissed:

Go in peace to love and serve the Lord.

We reply:

Thanks be to God.

Yes, indeed, we can go forth,
with our heart full of peace and joy,
because Jesus, our Risen Lord,
stays with us through his Spirit.

Listen with your heart
to what Jesus asks you:

*"Do you want to continue with me
the Great Story of love?"*

Continuing God's Great Story of love
means trying to live in communion
with other people and with God.
It means working to make our world
more beautiful and people happier.

**What answer are you going
to give Jesus?**

Each morning you can offer the new day that God gives you:

**Dear God, here I am!
With Jesus your Son,
I give you this day,
I give you my love
and with him I pray:
your kingdom may come!**

Dear parents:

This little book will help your child become familiar with the unfolding of the eucharist.

You will notice that ten pages are dedicated to the Proclamation of the Word, presenting in pictures and brief captions certain biblical stories. While enjoying these pages, the children will remain united to the community during that part of the celebration which is often long and difficult for them.

We would like to call your attention to the moments preceding and following Communion: they are of great significance in the child's personal relationship with Jesus. During these moments, which are sometimes distracting because of the coming and going in the congregation, you might help your child to pray quietly and personally with the book.

While a small amount of text has been included in this book, many of the congregational responses have been omitted. In a few cases one response has been chosen to indicate that a spoken reply is made. *The Book of Alternative Services* provides various options throughout the service, and encourages congregations to make use of its variety. You can help your child participate by showing him or her the appropriate responses in the *BAS* and connecting them with the pictures in this book.

The last three pages are meant to be read at home. Their aim is to encourage children to "live the eucharist" by loving God and caring for others in daily life, as we are all invited to do.

The intention of this book and the communion program, *Life in the Eucharist,* is to facilitate the participation of children in the eucharist and to aid liturgical renewal in the parish for all ages.

The National Children's Unit

Adapted by the Children's Unit of General Synod for use in the Anglican Church of Canada from *Come let us celebrate* by Françoise Darcy Bérubé and Jean-Paul Bérubé. This book has been adapted to comply with the text and theology of *The Book of Alternative Services of the Anglican Church of Canada* (1985).

Designed and illustrated by: Tiziana Tabbia-Plomteux

1986
Anglican Book Centre
600 Jarvis Street
Toronto, Ontario
Canada   M4Y 2J6

Copyright© 1986 by Anglican Book Centre and Françoise Darcy-Bérubé and Jean-Paul Bérubé.

All rights reserved. No parts of this book may be reproduced, stored in a retrieval system, or transmitted, in any form by any means, electronic, mechanical, photocopying, recording, or otherwise, without the written permission of the Anglican Book Centre.

Note: The biblical text on page 24 is a free adaptation for children of Luke 19:8-9.

Canadian Cataloguing in Publication Data
Main entry under title: The gift of life: children's book for the eucharist.
Adaptation of: Come let us celebrate, by Françoise Darcy-Bérubé and Jean-Paul Bérubé.

Adapted by the Children's Unit of General Synod for use with The book of alternative services of the Anglican Church of Canada.
ISBN 0-919891-62-4

1. Lord's Supper - Anglican Church of Canada - Juvenile literature.   2. Anglican Church of Canada - Liturgy - Texts - Juvenile literature.   3. Anglican Communion - Liturgy - Texts - Juvenile literature.   4. Children - Prayer-books and devotions - English

I.   Bérubé, Jean-Paul.   II. Tabbia-Plomteux, Tiziana.   III. Anglican Church of Canada. Children's Unit.   IV. Title.   V. Title: The book of alternative services of the Anglican Church of Canada.

BX5616.D37 1986   j264'.035   C86-094985-0